Anne Frank: The Diary of a Young Girl

Anne Frank

Abridged and adapted by Mark Falstein

Illustrated by Steve Moore

A PACEMAKER CLASSIC

GLOBE FEARON

Pearson Learning Group

Supervising Editor: Stephen Feinstein
Project Editor: Karen Bernhaut
Editorial Assistant: Stacie Dozier
Art Director: Nancy Sharkey
Assistant Art Director: Armando Baéz
Production Manager: Penny Gibson
Production Editor: Nicole Cypher
Desktop Specialist: Eric Dawson
Manufacturing Supervisor: Della Smith
Marketing Manager: Marge Curson
Cover Illustration: Steve Moore

This abridged version of *Anne Frank: The Diary of a Young Girl* is published by arrangement with Doubleday, a division of Bantam Doubleday Dell Publishing Group, Inc.

Printed in the United States of America
8 9 10 11 12   04 03 02 01
0-835-91066-0

Globe
Fearon

Pearson Learning Group

1-800-321-3106
www.pearsonlearning.com

Contents

Cast of Characters

In the Secret Annex

Anne Frank	A 13-year-old Jewish girl who keeps a diary while hiding from the Nazis
Otto Frank	Anne's father
Edith Frank	Anne's mother
Margot Frank	Anne's older sister
Mr. Van Daan	A Jewish businessman and Mr. Frank's associate
Mrs. Van Daan	Mr. Van Daan's wife
Peter Van Daan	The Van Daan's son
Mouschi	Peter Van Daan's cat

Anne's School Friends

Lies Goosen	Anne's best friend
Jopie De Waal	Anne's friend in Jewish High School
Peter Wessel	The boy Anne has a crush on
Harry Goldberg	Anne's older boyfriend

Dutch Protectors

Mr. Koophuis	One of Mr. Frank's business associates
Mr. Kraler	Another of Mr. Frank's business associates
Miep and Henk Van Santen	Good friends of the Frank family
Elli Vossen	A typist in Mr. Frank's business office

1 Going Into Hiding

Sunday, 14 June, 1942

Friday was my birthday. The first present that greeted me was you. I got lots of things from Mother and Daddy. I got a few books, a game, a brooch, and some money. Now I can buy *The Myths of Greece and Rome*—great! Then Lies came over, and we went to school. Now I must stop. Bye-bye, you and I are going to be great friends!

Monday, 15 June, 1942

I had my birthday party on Sunday afternoon. There were lots of girls and boys. Mother always wants to know whom I'm going to marry. Little does she guess that it's Peter Wessel! For years Lies Goosens has been my best friend. But since I've been at Jewish High School, I've gotten to know Jopie de Waal. She is now my best friend. And Lies is more friendly with another girl.

Saturday, 20 June, 1942

I haven't written for a few days. I wanted to think about my diary. It's odd for me to keep a diary. I've never had one before. It seems to me that no one—myself included—would care about the thoughts of a 13-year-old girl. Still, what does that matter? I want to write. I want to bring out the things that lie deep in my heart. I don't plan to show this diary to anyone until I find a real friend. And that is the reason I am starting this diary—I have no such friend.

Of course I am not alone in the world. I have dear parents and a 16-year-old sister. I have many people that I call friends. I have strings of boyfriends. But with all of them it's just fun and joking. We never seem to talk about anything that really matters. Maybe it's because I'm not sure of myself. Anyway, I can't do anything about it.

And so this diary. I want this diary to be my friend, and I will call my friend Kitty. It won't do to begin my letters to Kitty just out of the blue. So here, in short, is the story of my life:

My father was 36 when he married my mother. She was 25. My sister Margot was born in 1926 in Frankfurt, Germany. I came along on June 12, 1929. Because we are Jewish, we moved to Holland in 1933.

The rest of our family stayed in Germany and has really suffered. In 1938, two uncles escaped to the United States. In May 1940, bad times began here. The Germans took over Holland. They passed one anti-Jewish law after another. Jews must wear a yellow star. Jews cannot own bicycles. Jews may not ride the streetcar or drive a car. Jews can only shop between three and five o'clock. Jews must not be out after eight o'clock, even in their own gardens. Jews may not take part in sports. Jews may not visit Christians. Jews must go to Jewish schools. And so on.

But life goes on. So far, everything is all right with the four of us. And here I come to the present day.

Wednesday, 24 June, 1942

Dear Kitty,

It is boiling hot. Now I can appreciate how nice a streetcar is. Jews are allowed on the ferry, and that's about all. I have to walk all the way to school. Thank goodness, vacation begins next week.

Monday I met a boy named Harry Goldberg at my friend Eva's house. Yesterday he was waiting for me on my way to school. Harry is 16. He tells all kinds of funny stories. He was waiting for me again this morning. I think he will be from now on.

Tuesday, 30 June, 1942

Dear Kitty,

Harry and I have gotten to know each other well in a week. He has told me a lot about his life. He came to Holland alone. He is living with his grandparents. His parents are in Belgium.

It's easy to see that Harry is in love with me. It's rather fun for a change. His grandmother thinks I'm too young to be seeing him so often. But my family approves of him. He likes them too, but he thinks my girlfriends are very childish. He's right.

Sunday morning, 5 July, 1942

Dear Kitty,

Our exam results were announced on Friday. My report card was not all bad. But I could do better in math. My parents don't care about my grades as long as I'm happy and not too fresh. I am just the opposite. I want to be a good student. Margot got her report card too—brilliant as usual. She's so brainy.

Daddy has been home a lot lately. There is nothing for him to do at work. It must be rotten for him to feel so useless. Mr. Koophuis and Mr. Kraler have taken over his food business. A few days ago, Daddy began to talk of us going into hiding.

"Yes, Anne," he said. "You know that we have been taking our belongings to friends for more than a year. We don't want them to be seized by the Germans, and we certainly don't want to be taken by them ourselves. So we shall disappear and not wait until they come for us."

"But Daddy, when will it be?" I asked. He spoke so seriously that it scared me.

"Don't worry about it, we shall arrange everything. Make the best use of your carefree young life while you can."

That was all. Oh, I hope it doesn't happen soon!

Wednesday, 8 July, 1942

Dear Kitty,

Years seem to have passed since Sunday. So much has happened! My world has been turned upside down. But I am alive, and that is the main thing.

On Sunday, the S.S. sent a call-up notice for Margot. It was a great shock. Everyone knows what a call-up means—concentration camps. Mother went to tell the Van Daans right away. Mr. Van Daan works with Daddy in the business. They decided that we would go into hiding together at once. Margot and I packed some of our things into a school bag. I packed this diary, hair curlers, a comb, books, old letters—the craziest things.

Daddy asked Mr. Koophuis to be at the office that evening. Van Daan went and got Miep Van Santen and her husband Henk. Miep has worked for Daddy since 1933. She and Henk are our close friends. They put more of our things in their pockets and went away.

The next day we awoke early. It was warm, but we all wore several layers of clothes. No Jew would dare walk through the streets carrying a suitcase. We left the apartment a mess. This was to let people think that we had left without plans. We didn't care about the mess. We only wanted to get away. More tomorrow.

Thursday, 9 July, 1942

Dear Kitty,

We walked through the pouring rain. Daddy told me a little about the plan. The hiding place would be at his business. The offices are on the first floor. There are storerooms in the front part of the second floor. On the other side of the stairs is a door hidden by a cupboard. Behind this door is a steep staircase. It leads to a few tiny rooms in the back. This is where our family will live. Margot and I will share a room. Another staircase leads to a third floor. There is a large room with a stove and a sink. This will be our kitchen, living room, and dining room. Next to it is the Van Daans' bedroom. Peter Van Daan will

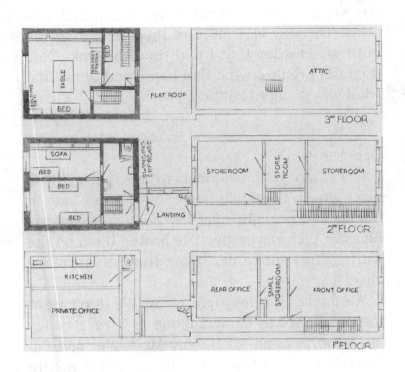

have a tiny little corridor room. There, now you know all about our beautiful "Secret Annex."

When we got here Monday, all the rooms were full of trash. There were cardboard boxes full of our things. Daddy had had them sent to the office—he'd been planning this for months! All day we unpacked, cleaned up, and put things away. Tuesday was more of the same. It wasn't until Wednesday that I had time to think. Only then did I realize what had happened to me and what was going to happen.

Saturday, 11 July, 1942

Dear Kitty,

I can't say yet how it feels to "disappear." This place doesn't feel like home, but I don't hate it. Daddy had brought over my postcards and my film-star pictures earlier. I've pasted them on the walls. They make my room look much more cheerful.

We made curtains right away. We don't want the neighbors to know anyone is here. Besides Mr. Koophuis and Miep, only Mr. Kraler and Elli Vossen know about us. Elli, a typist in the business, is 23. We can make no sound, or other people might hear us. Margot has a cold, but she is not allowed to cough.

The Van Daans arrive on Tuesday. It should be more fun then, and not so quiet. The silence scares me, especially at night. It is terrible never to be able to go outside. I'm afraid that we might be discovered and shot.

I must go. Someone is calling me.

2 Life with the Van Daans

Friday, 14 August, 1942

Dear Kitty,

I haven't written for a whole month. Honestly, so little happens here that I can't find anything interesting to tell you.

The Van Daans arrived a day early. The Germans were calling up so many people that they decided to play it safe. Peter Van Daan is 15. He is a rather soft, shy, gawky boy. I can't expect much from his company. He brought his cat, Mouschi.

After three days we were like one large, cozy family. Mr. Van Daan told us that we fooled everyone. The Germans think we have left the country. One family thinks they saw us go by on bicycles early one morning. Another neighbor is sure that a German army car came for us in the middle of the night.

Friday, 21 August, 1942

Dear Kitty,

I'm not working much right now. I'm giving myself a vacation until September. Then Daddy is going to be my teacher. There is little change in our life here. Mr. Van Daan and I usually manage to upset each other. He likes Margot very much, however. Mother sometimes treats me like a baby, which I can't stand. I still think Peter is boring. He spends most of his time in bed. What a fool!

Wednesday, 2 September, 1942

Dear Kitty,

Mr. and Mrs. Van Daan had a huge argument. I've never seen anything like it. Mother and Daddy would never yell at each other like that. The cause was so trivial, it was just a waste of breath. Still, everyone to his own liking.

It is not all honey between Mother and Mrs. Van Daan. Mrs. Van Daan took her sheets out of the cupboard. She doesn't want us using them. She also doesn't like it that we're using her dinner plates and not ours. Yesterday I broke one of her soup bowls. "Oh!" she cried, "couldn't you be careful for once? That's the last one I've got!"

Mother gave me another sermon this morning. Our views are completely opposite. Daddy is a dear, but he gets angry with me, too. Last week we had a big to-do in our dull lives. It had to do with a book about women—and Peter. Usually Margot and Peter are allowed to read all the books Mr. Koophuis lends us. But the adults decided that this book was not right for Peter. Of course he got hold of it. He read it secretly in the attic. Then Peter's father caught him with the book. He sent him to bed without his supper. Peter sulked off to sleep in the attic. The next morning, Daddy patched things up with a few kind words. After a few days, everything was peaceful again.

Monday, 21 September, 1942

Dear Kitty,

I can't stand Mrs. Van Daan. I get nothing but blow-ups from her. She thinks I talk too much. Now she's making up excuses to get out of washing the pans when it's her turn.

I'm busy with Daddy working out his family tree. As we go along, he tells me a little about everyone. It's most interesting. Mr. Koophuis brings a few special books for me every other week.

School time has come again. My favorite subject is history. We brought a lot of school books and supplies with us. I'm working hard at my French. Peter sighs and groans over his English.

The adults were talking about me. They decided that I wasn't completely stupid after all. Of course, that made me work extra hard the next day.

I was just writing something about Mrs. Van Daan when in she came. Slap! I closed the book. She wanted to take a peek anyway, but I wouldn't let her. It gave me quite a shock!

Sunday, September 27, 1942

Dear Kitty,

Just had another big blow-up with Mother. We just don't get along these days. It's not going too well between Margot and me either. We usually don't yell much in our family, but lately Margot and Mother are getting on my nerves.

The Van Daans love to talk about other people's children. Margot doesn't mind; she is such a goody-goody. I, however, seem to have enough mischief in me for two. The Van Daans think I'm spoiled. They are always quick to let Mother and Daddy know it. My parents always defend me. But they do tell me I shouldn't talk so much or poke my nose into everything. If Daddy weren't so sweet, I'd be afraid I was a disappointment to them.

Monday, 28 September, 1942

Dear Kitty,

Why do grown-ups quarrel so much, and over the stupidest things? I used to think it was only children who had quarrels. Of course grown-ups call them "discussions." I suppose I should get used to it. But I can't, not as long as nearly every discussion is about me! Nothing about me is right. They talk about the way I look, my character, my manners. I'm just supposed to take it and keep quiet. But I can't! I'll show them! Maybe they'll keep their mouths shut when I start educating them. I am amazed at their awful manners and especially by Mrs. Van Daan's stupidity.

Kitty, if only you knew how angry they make me! I shall just explode one day!

Tuesday, 29 September, 1942

Dear Kitty,

When people are in hiding, they find ways to get by. We have no bath, so we use a washtub.

The only hot water is on the bottom floor, and we all take turns using it. Everyone has his or her own favorite place for bathing. Peter uses the kitchen. Mr. Van Daan carries his hot water all the way upstairs to his room. Mrs. Van Daan hasn't bathed at all. She is waiting to see which is the best place. Daddy uses the private office, Mother the kitchen. Margot and I have chosen the front office.

Last week, a plumber was here for three days. That was hard. We were unable to get water or use the toilet all day. Even harder was having to be silent. Usually we have to whisper, but not being able to talk at all was ten times worse.

Friday, October 9, 1942

Dear Kitty,

The news from outside is very bad. Our Jewish friends are being taken away by the dozens. They are loaded into cattle cars and sent to a concentration camp at Westerbork. From there they are sent away to. . . where? We think that most of them are killed. The English radio says they are being gassed.

Maybe that is the quickest way to die. I am very upset. I had to listen while Miep told these awful stories. Recently, she said, a poor old Jewish woman was sitting on her doorstep. The Gestapo had told her to wait there while they got a car to take her away. The poor old thing was so frightened! But Miep did not dare take her in. No one would take such a chance. It is not the Dutch people's fault that the Germans have no mercy.

To think that I was once a German, too! Now I have no country. Hitler took that away from us long ago. Now Germans and Jews are the greatest enemies in the world.

3 Taking in Another Person

Tuesday, 20 October, 1942

Dear Kitty,

My hand is still shaking! We knew that a carpenter would be coming to fill the fire extinguishers. But we didn't know when. So we didn't even try to be quiet today. When we suddenly heard him hammering near the cupboard that hides our door, we became very quiet. Then we thought he started knocking on the door! Had he heard us after all? It seemed like he was pounding and pulling at the cupboard.

Just when I thought we had been discovered, I heard Mr. Koophuis say, "Open the door, it's me." We opened it at once. The hook that holds the cupboard closed, which can only be undone by people who know the secret, had gotten stuck. That was why Mr. Koophuis hadn't warned us about the carpenter earlier. So it was only a bad scare.

Dear Kitty,

Mother is in a bad mood. That always means problems for me. Is it just chance that she and Daddy never scold Margot and always dump on me for everything? Just last evening I picked up a book Margot had been reading. When Margot came back into the room, she had this look. She asked for "her" book back. Just because I wanted to look at it a little while longer, she got angry. Then Mother jumped in. "Give the book to Margot; she was reading it," she said. Then Daddy came in. He didn't even know what it was about, but he took Margot's side. I put the book down and left the room. They thought I was angry, but it was only that my feelings were hurt.

I knew Mother would stick up for Margot. She always takes her side. I'm so used to it that I don't care any more. I love them, but only because they are my mother and sister.

With Daddy, it's different. He's the one I look up to. He doesn't notice that he treats Margot differently from me. I have always been second-best. I have always had to pay double for anything I did wrong. First I am scolded and then my feelings get hurt. I won't take it any more. I want something from Daddy that he is not able to give me.

I'm not jealous of Margot. It's only that I long for Daddy's real love. I don't want him to love me just as his child, but as Anne, myself.

Only through Daddy can I feel the least bit of family feeling. He doesn't like it when I talk about Mother's failings. He doesn't want to hear about it. Just the same, I find her failings harder to take than anything else. I don't like always having to call attention to how mean and sloppy she is. But I just can't keep it all to myself. I wish I could only see Mother's good side. But it doesn't work. Neither she nor Daddy understands this empty space in my life. I wonder if parents can ever make their children happy.

Sometimes I think that God wants to test me. I must become good on my own, with no one to be an example for me. Then later on it will make me stronger. From whom but myself will I get comfort? I need comforting. My faults are too great. I know this, and every day I try to make myself better.

The way they treat me changes so much. One day they think I'm grown up. The next day I hear that Anne is just a silly little goat. She doesn't know anything. I'm not a baby any more. I'm not to be laughed at. I have my own plans and ideas, even though I can't put them into words yet. I'm tired of having no one who understands me. That is why in the end I always come back to my diary, because Kitty is always patient. I'll promise her that I'll be strong. I'll find my own way through it all, without crying. I only wish I could sometimes hear a kind word from someone who loves me.

Monday, 9 November, 1942

Dear Kitty,

Yesterday was Peter's sixteenth birthday. He got some nice presents. Among them were a Monopoly game and a lighter. He doesn't smoke; it's just for show.

The biggest surprise came from Mr. Van Daan. He told us that the British have landed in northern Africa. "This is the beginning of the end," everyone was saying. But Churchill, the British prime minister, said, "This is not the end. It is not even the beginning of the end. But it is, perhaps, the end of the beginning." Do you see the difference? There is reason for hope now.

But to return to our hiding place. I must tell you something about our food supply. As you know, we have some real greedy pigs on the top floor. We get our bread from a friend of Koophuis. We don't get as much as we used to at home, but it's enough. We also have four illegal ration cards. Their price keeps going up all the time. We also have lots of canned vegetables and six sacks of dried beans. The sacks weigh about 50 pounds each. Peter was given the job of dragging them upstairs. He was just pulling up the last one when it split open. The beans poured out and went rattling down the stairs! Thank goodness there were no strangers in the house! Peter was scared at first. But when he saw me standing up to my ankles in beans, he started roaring with laughter. I was an island in a sea of beans! We still haven't gotten them all picked up.

Tuesday, 10 November, 1942

Dear Kitty,

Great news—we are taking in another person. We have always thought we had enough food and room. We just didn't want to give Koophuis and Kraler more trouble. But when Daddy asked them, they said, "It is just as dangerous for seven as it is for eight." The man who will be joining us is a dentist, Albert Dussel. We all knew him before the war. His wife was lucky enough to be out of the country when the war started. He is quiet and, as far as we know, he is a pleasant person. He will have to share my room instead of Margot, who will use a cot.

Tuesday, 17 November, 1942

Dear Kitty,

Dussel has arrived. All went well. Miep arranged for him to be at the post office at 11 o'clock, where Mr. Koophuis would meet him. Mr. Koophuis sent him to Miep at the office. She had him take off his coat, so that his yellow star could not be seen. Then she brought him into the private office until the cleaning woman went home. At last she showed him upstairs.

He was speechless when Miep opened the swinging cupboard. When he saw us, I thought he was going to pass out! He just fell into a chair and stared. "But I thought—" he stammered. "Aren't you in Belgium? Didn't you escape?" We explained everything to him. He explored our beautiful little "Secret Annex." Then we all had lunch together. After a nap and some tea, he started to feel more at home.

Friday, 20 November, 1942

Dear Kitty

Dussel is a very nice man. Of course, he thought it was all right to share my little room. I'm not so happy about it myself, but one sometimes has to give things up for a good cause. "If we can save someone, that is all that's important," Daddy says, and he's right.

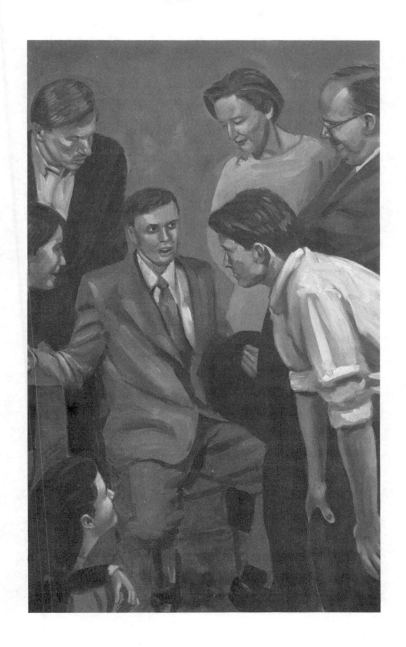

The first day Dussel was here, he asked all sorts of questions. When does the cleaning woman come? When can one take a bath? When can one use the toilet? These things are not so simple in a hiding place. I explained it all to Dussel, but he's a little slow to catch on. He has to ask everything twice, and even then he forgets. Maybe it's only that he's upset by the sudden change.

Dussel has told us a lot about what's going on outside. The Jews are being rounded up. The Germans ring every door and ask whether there are any Jews living in the house. If there are, the whole family is taken away at once. I often see rows of them being pushed along the street—old people, sick people, crying babies.

How lucky we are in our hiding place! I feel wicked sleeping in a warm bed. I get frightened when I think of our friends who have been taken away to be killed. And all because they are Jews!

None of us really knows how to take it all. Until now, we thought it best to remain as cheerful as possible. But Dussel's stories are so awful that I can't get them out of my mind.

Yet it won't do us any good to go on being gloomy. It won't help those outside either. Must I feel ashamed for laughing and being cheerful?

4 Living in Darkness

Saturday, 28 November, 1942

Dear Kitty,

We have used too much electricity, more than our ration. Now we must do without light for two weeks. It's too dark to read after four o'clock. We pass the time in funny ways. We tell riddles. We exercise in the dark. We discuss books. We practice our English and French. Last night I was peeking with field glasses into the houses behind us. I never knew that neighbors could be so interesting.

I always heard that Dr. Dussel got on well with children. But now I know the truth. He's old-fashioned and set in his ways. He gives long, dull sermons on manners. Worse yet, he's a tattle-tale. He's always telling on me to Mother. So first I get it from him, and then I get it from her. And if I'm really lucky, I get it from Mrs. Van Daan, too.

Don't think it's easy being the "badly brought-up" child of a family in hiding! I hear so much about my faults I don't know whether to laugh or cry!

Monday, 7 December, 1942

Dear Kitty,

Chanukah and Christmas came just a day apart this year. We didn't do much for Chanukah. We just gave each other a few presents. We lit the candles but, because they are so hard to get, we only had them burning for ten minutes.

Christmas was fun. Miep and Elli surprised us with a party. There were presents for everyone. None of us had ever celebrated Christmas, and it was a nice way to start.

Wednesday, 13 January, 1943

Dear Kitty,

Everything has upset me again this morning. I wasn't able to finish a single thing properly.

It is terrible outside. Every day, more people are dragged off. Families are torn apart. Children come home from school and find that their parents have disappeared. Women come home from shopping to find their homes shut up and their families gone.

The Dutch people are worried, too. Their sons are being sent to Germany. Everyone is afraid.

Every night hundreds of planes fly over on their way to Germany. The ground is torn up by their bombs. Every hour thousands of people are killed. The whole world is at war. Even though our side is winning, the end is not in sight.

We are luckier than most people. It is quiet and safe here. Yet we are so selfish! We talk about "after the war." We brighten up at the thought of new clothes. We ought to save every penny to help other people who are suffering!

The children around here are cold and starving. They beg for bread. There is nothing we can do but wait calmly until it is over. Jews and Christians wait. The whole world waits, and there are many who wait for death.

Saturday, 30 January, 1943

Dear Kitty,

I'm boiling with rage, and yet I must not show it. I'd like to cry, scream, and stamp my feet. I'd like to give Mother a good shaking for all the nasty words and ugly looks I get day after day.

I would like to shout at all of them—Margot, Van Daan, Dussel—even Daddy. I want to shout, "Leave me alone! Let me sleep just one night without crying! Let me get away from it all, away from the world!" But I can't do that. They must not know how I feel. I can't let them see how they hurt me. They would act so sorry and make kindly jokes. That would make me want to scream even more. If I talk, they think I'm showing off. If I'm quiet, they think I'm stupid. I'm rude if I answer back. I'm sly if I get a good idea. I'm lazy if I'm tired. I'm selfish if I eat a mouthful more than I should. And so on, and so on. I laugh about it and pretend I don't mind, but I do mind. I am the way I am. I try my best to please everyone, but just once I'd like to give back to them what they make me feel. Oh, if only I could!

Wednesday, 10 March, 1943

Dear Kitty,

The electricity went out again last night. On top of that, the guns keep banging away. I creep into Daddy's bed nearly every night. I know it's very childish, but you don't know what it's like. The guns are so loud you can't hear yourself talk. Mrs. Van Daan, who claims that she accepts whatever happens, is the most scared of all.

Have I told you about Mrs. Van Daan's fears? One night she thought there were burglars in the attic. She heard footsteps, and she was so scared that she woke her husband. She was afraid they would steal our food. A few nights later, the whole Van Daan family was awakened by spooky sounds. Peter went to the attic with a flashlight. What do you think it was? A swarm of huge rats! When we knew who the burglars were, we let Mouschi sleep in the attic. They didn't come back again, at least not at night.

Thursday, 25 March, 1943

Dear Kitty,

Yesterday I was sitting with my family when Peter came in. He whispered something to Daddy. I heard something about "a barrel falling over downstairs," and "someone making noise at the door." Daddy and Peter went down at once.

Meanwhile, the rest of us crept quietly up to the third floor. Soon Daddy and Peter appeared again. They were white to the roots of their hair. They said they thought that someone had broken into the house!

The worst part was that we left the radio on downstairs. If the door was broken in, a passer-by might notice and call the police. They would surely hear the radio, and then things would be all over for us. The men went down to check things again. The rest of us waited in suspense until they came back and told us that all was quiet.

We all went to bed, but none of us could sleep. This morning the men went downstairs to see if the outside door had been broken open. It had not. We were safe. We told Koophuis and the others what had happened. They all made fun of it. It is easy to laugh at such things afterwards. Elli was the only one who took us seriously.

Friday, April 2, 1943

Dear Kitty,

Oh dear, I've done it again. I was lying in bed last night waiting for Daddy. He always joins me in prayers and wishes me good night. Then Mother came in. She sat on the bed and said very nicely, "Anne, Daddy can't come yet. Shall I say your prayers with you tonight?"

"No, Mother," I answered.

Mother got up. She walked slowly to the door. Suddenly she turned around. She looked very upset. She said, "I don't want to be angry. Love cannot be forced." She was crying as she left the room.

I felt horrible to push her away. But I knew that I could not have said anything else. I felt very sorry for Mother. For the first time I could see that she minds my coldness. But she herself has pushed me away with her cruel remarks. Just as she has hurt me, so she is hurt to know that all the love between us is gone. She cried half the night.

She and Daddy expect me to apologize, but I can't. I spoke the truth. Mother would have to know it sooner or later. I can only feel sorry for her. But I won't hide the truth from them any longer. The longer it is put off, the harder it will be for them when they do hear it.

5 Burglars and Bombings

Tuesday, 27 April, 1943

Dear Kitty,

The Carlton Hotel is smashed to bits. Two British planes filled with bombs fell on the German Officers' Club. None of us can sleep. I have dark circles under my eyes. Our food is awful. Breakfast is dry bread and coffee. Dinner is spinach or lettuce for two weeks straight.

All the men who fought in the Dutch army in 1940 have been called up to work for Hitler as prisoners of war. I suppose that's in case of invasion.

Saturday, 1 May, 1943

Dear Kitty,

I know that our life here is wonderful compared with how other Jews are living. But when it's all over, I know I'll be amazed to think of how we sank to such a low level. Everything is dirty. All our clothes are wearing out. And we used to be so neat!

Of course these are all things we can live with. But sometimes I wonder how we are ever going to get back to normal.

Tuesday, 18 May, 1943

Dear Kitty,

I saw a huge air battle between British and German planes. Some of the men on our side had to jump from their burning planes. Our milkman saw four of them sitting by the road. The German police came and took them away.

It is getting warm. Still, we have to light our fires every other day in order to burn garbage. If we put it in garbage cans, someone would notice. How easily we could be caught if we were careless!

Tuesday, 15 June, 1943

Dear Kitty,

Daddy wrote me a sweet poem for my birthday. I got some lovely things. One was a fat book on my favorite subject—the myths of Greece and Rome. There were also a lot of sweets. Everyone broke into their last reserves. As the youngest of our family in hiding, I am more honored than I deserve.

We must hand in our radio next month. Koophuis has a small, secret one at home that he will let us use. It is a shame to have to hand in our big one, but one can't take any chances of getting caught. The radio has been our source of courage. It helps us say, "Chins up. Better times will come."

Sunday, 11 July, 1943

Dear Kitty,

We are back on the "upbringing" theme again. I really am trying to be helpful and polite. It is very hard to be on such good behavior with people you can't stand. But I really do see that I get along better by pretending a little.

Margot and I have been studying shorthand. Now I have to let it go a bit. I need more time for my other subjects, and I am also having trouble with my eyes. I have needed glasses for a long time. (Yuck, I would look like an owl!) Yesterday Mother talked about sending me to the eye doctor with Mrs. Koophuis. Imagine it! Going outside on the street! But I don't think it will happen. Now that the British have landed in Sicily, Daddy is hoping for a "quick finish."

Elli gives Margot and me a lot of office work. It makes us both feel very useful, and it is a big help to her. We take special care to do a good job.

Miep is just like a pack mule. Almost every day she finds some vegetables for us. She brings them on her bicycle. We long for Saturdays, when our books come. It's just like getting a present. People outside don't know what books mean to us. Reading, learning, and the radio are our fun.

Dear Kitty,

There is a small writing table in my room. I sit there every day from 2:30 until 4:00 while Dussel sleeps. Yesterday afternoon, I asked Dussel if he might let me use it until 5:30 two afternoons a week. I asked Daddy's permission, and I was very polite. Now, what do you think the learned Dussel said? "No." Just plain "No!" I refused to be put off like that. I asked him the reason for his answer. What he told me was this: "I have to work, too. If I can't work in the afternoons, there is no time left for me at all. If I start a job, I have to finish it that day, or else I've done all the work for nothing. Anyway, you don't work seriously at anything. I am at the table, and I shall stay there."

I said, "Dr. Dussel, I do work seriously. There is nowhere else for me to go in the afternoon. In the common room there is too much going on. I ask you kindly to think about it again."

With these words I turned my back on the learned doctor. I was so angry! I thought Dussel was very rude. Later, when I was calmer, I tried again. I said, "When you first came here, we agreed that this room would be for both of us. If we were fair, you would have the morning and I all the afternoon. But I don't even ask that much. I don't see why two afternoons a week should be a problem."

At this Dussel jumped up as if someone had stuck him with a pin. "You can't talk about your rights here at all. Where am I supposed to go? I simply can't work anywhere. You are so selfish! You don't mind pushing everyone else to the side. I've never seen such a child! If your sister asked me for such a thing, of course I would say yes. But you. . ."

It went on and on. Finally I ran to Daddy. I told him the whole story. He told me that he and Dussel had already discussed the subject once. He had pretended to take Dussel's side. He did not want to put him in the wrong in front of the young. But Daddy had not thought it fair then. This time he stuck up for me. He got Dussel to give in. Now Dussel is not speaking to me—how childish!

Friday, 16 July, 1943

Dear Kitty,

Burglars again—real ones this time! This morning Peter discovered that the doors had been forced open. He told Daddy, who tuned the

radio in the private office to Germany and locked the door.

Everyone stayed perfectly silent all morning. Later we learned from Mr. Koophuis that the burglars had not found much to steal. But they did take all our coupons for sugar.

Monday, 19 July, 1943

Dear Kitty,

North Amsterdam was very heavily bombed on Sunday. Whole streets lie in ruins. It will be a long time before all the people are dug out. Children are lost, looking for their parents. I shudder when I hear the dull, droning rumble in the distance. It means that destruction is coming near.

Friday, 23 July, 1943

Dear Kitty,

Just for fun, I'm going to tell you everyone's first wish when we can go outside again. Margot and Mr. Van Daan long for a hot bath. Mrs. Van Daan wants ice cream. Dussel thinks only of seeing his wife. Mother wants a cup of coffee. Daddy is going to visit a friend in the hospital. Peter wants to go to a movie. I would find it so blissful, I wouldn't know where to start! I long to be home, to be able to move freely, to be back in school.

Monday, 26 July, 1943

Dear Kitty,

Nothing but uproar and excitement yesterday. We heard the first warning siren while we were at breakfast. We don't care about that, it only means that planes are crossing the coast.

It was after two o'clock that the sirens began to wail again. All at once the guns began shooting hard. The house shook. Then down came the bombs. Before long you could smell burning. From the window upstairs I could see columns of smoke rising. Then in the evening, there was another air raid.

I had an "escape bag" packed, but there is nowhere to go. It is just as dangerous for us in the street as in a bombing raid. The guns did not stop firing until two in the morning.

Seven o'clock. I sat up in bed with a start. Mr. Van Daan was talking. Wonderful news, perhaps the best in all the war years. "Mussolini has fallen. The King of Italy has taken over the government." We jumped for joy. At last there is hope. Hope for it to end, hope for peace— perhaps even this year.

6 A Typical Day in the Secret Annex

Wednesday, 4 August, 1943

Dear Kitty,

We have now been in the "Secret Annex" for over a year. There is so much to tell. Everything is so different from ordinary times and from ordinary people's lives. To give you a closer look, I'm going to describe a typical day. Today, I'm beginning with the evening.

9:00 P.M. Going to bed in the "Secret Annex" is quite a business. Chairs are pushed around, beds are pulled out. Nothing stays where it is during the day. There is much noise as beds are moved into place. I sleep on a couch. It is so short that chairs must be used to lengthen it.

I use the bathroom after Peter has his turn. I have half an hour to wash, brush my teeth, put my hair up, and do everything else.

10:00. Good night! For a while there is a creaking of beds and a sighing of broken springs. Soon all is quiet, that is if the Van Daans don't quarrel in bed upstairs.

11:30. The bathroom door creaks. A strip of light falls into the room. A squeak of shoes, a large coat. Dussel returns from his night work in

Kraler's office. He shuffles and makes up his bed. Then his shadow disappears again, and all is quiet.

3:00. I get up to go to the bathroom. Then I lie awake for a while, listening to the night sounds. Dussel makes noises like a fish gasping for breath. Sometimes there is also some shooting in the night. When that happens I run like a little girl to Daddy's bed.

6:45. Trrrrr—the alarm clock rings. Crack—ping—Mrs. Van Daan has turned it off. Creak—Mr. Van Daan gets up, puts on water, and then runs to the bathroom. A new day has begun.

Thursday, 5 August, 1943

Dear Kitty,

Today I am going to describe lunchtime.

12:30. We can all breathe. The warehouse workers have gone home for lunch. Above, one can hear Mrs. Van Daan's vacuum cleaner. Margot goes off to help Dussel with his Dutch lesson. Daddy takes a book into a corner and tries to find some peace. Mother goes upstairs to help the busy housewife. I go to the bathroom to clean it up a bit, and myself, too.

12:45. The place is filling up. First Mr. Van Santen, then Koophuis or Kraler come in. Elli visits, and sometimes Miep, as well.

1:00. We sit around the little radio, listening to the BBC. This is the only time we do not interrupt one another—not even Mr. Van Daan. Then comes the great share-out. Everyone has a little soup. Mr. Van Santen reads the newspaper. Koophuis tells us the latest news from town.

1:45. We all go about our own business. There follows the most peaceful hour. Dussel sleeps, and I go to my work. The time goes fast. At four o'clock the doctor is standing beside me. He holds the clock to show me I'm one minute late in clearing the table for him.

Dear Kitty,

Going on with our daily routine, I shall now describe the evening meal:

Mr. Van Daan begins. He is first to be served and takes a lot of everything he likes. Usually he talks at the same time. He gives his views on everything. Of course his are the only views worth listening to. All right, he is smart, but he gets high marks for being full of himself.

Madame Van Daan. When she's in one of her moods, you can't look at her. She is the one who starts all the arguments. At the table, she's picky. The others will get their share, as long as she gets the best. Then she talks—whether or not anyone is listening.

Young Mr. Van Daan. One doesn't hear much from him. As for his appetite, he is never full. After the biggest meal, he says he could have eaten double.

Number four—Margot. Eats like a mouse and doesn't talk at all. "Spoiled" is what the Van Daans like to say. "Not enough fresh air" is what we think.

Beside her—Mother. Eats well; talks much.

Numbers six and seven. I won't say much about Daddy and me. He looks first to see if everyone else has something. He needs nothing himself; the best things are for the children. Sitting beside him is me, the "Secret Annex's" bundle of nerves.

Finally—Dr. Dussel. Helps himself, never looks up, eats, and doesn't talk.

Friday, 29 October, 1943

Dear Kitty,

There have been loud arguments again between the Van Daans. They have run out of money. Van Daan got the idea of selling his wife's fur coat. A friend of Koophuis's paid a lot of money for it. However, Mrs. Van Daan wanted to keep the money to buy new clothes after the war. Mr. Van Daan made it clear that it was needed to buy food right now.

The yells, screams, stamping and name-calling—you can't imagine it! It's very upsetting. At night I fall into bed crying. I thank heaven that I sometimes have half an hour to myself.

I'm not eating much. I keep being told that I don't look well. There is a heavy feeling here, especially on Sundays. You don't hear a single bird singing outside. The silence grabs me as if it will drag me under. At such times I wander from room to room. I feel like a bird hurling myself against the bars of a cage. I sleep to make the time pass more quickly, and the quiet and the fear. There is no way of killing them.

Monday evening, 9 November, 1943

Dear Kitty,

My letters to you seem to be written in so many different moods! Our feelings all change so much here. Lately, you may have noticed, I'm depressed. I really couldn't tell you why. I think it's just because I'm a coward.

At night, in bed, I see myself alone in a dungeon. Sometimes our "Secret Annex" is on fire, or they come to take us away at night. I see it all as if it is really happening. I can't believe that the world will ever be normal for us again. I talk about "after the war," but it is something that will never really happen. I think back to our old house, my friends, the fun at school. It is as if another person lived it all, not me.

Saturday, 27 November, 1943

Dear Kitty.

Last night, before I fell asleep, Lies appeared before my eyes! She was dressed in rags. Her face was thin. Her eyes were very big and sad. I could read in her eyes, "Oh, Anne, why have you left me? Help me, oh, help me. Rescue me from this hell!"

I cannot help her. I can only look on as others suffer and die. I pray to God to send her back. She was my best friend, and I did her a great wrong. I was too young to understand her feelings. She had become friends with another girl, and to her it seemed that I wanted to take her away. Now she looks at me so helplessly with that pale face and those begging eyes. If only I could help her!

Why should I be chosen to live and she to die? What was the difference between us? Why are we so far from each other now?

Oh, Lies, if you live to the end of the war, I hope that you will come back to us. I want to make up for the wrong I did you.

I shall never forget her again, and I shall always pray for her.

7 Growing Up

Friday, 24 December, 1943

Dear Kitty,

I have had the flu. That's why I haven't written for a while. It's awful to be sick here. But I'm fine again, a little taller and heavier, and with a real appetite for learning.

We are all getting on well together for once! There is no quarreling. We haven't had such peace here for at least half a year.

For the second time in my life I have received a Christmas present. Koophuis, Kraler, and the girls prepared a lovely surprise again. Miep has made a beautiful cake, on which is written "Peace 1944."

I think of how lucky we are compared with other Jews. But believe me, being shut up for a year and a half can get to be too much. You can't crush your feelings. I have a great longing to have lots of fun. I want to laugh until I ache. I want to smell fresh air. Cycling, dancing, feeling free—that's what I long for. Still, I must not show it. Where would it lead us if we started to pity ourselves? If I talked about it to anyone, I know I would cry. Crying can bring such relief.

Sunday, 2 January, 1944

Dear Kitty,

Today I read over some of the early pages in this diary. I was shocked at the way I talked about Mother.

I have been trying to understand the Anne of a year ago. I suffer from moods that keep my head under water, so to speak. In those moods, I can see only my own point of view.

I hid inside myself. I wrote down all my feelings in this diary. It has become a great treasure to me. But I can see now that there are many pages I would rather put behind me.

I used to get so angry with Mother. I still do sometimes. It's true that she doesn't understand me, but I don't understand her either. She loves me very much. It's just because things are so hard here that she snapped at me. I felt that she didn't respect me. But I can see now that in a normal life we could have worked things out.

The time when I made Mother cry is over. I'm just glad that most of my angry words for her are on paper. It's better than knowing she carries them in her heart.

Wednesday, 5 January, 1944

Dear Kitty,

I have something on my mind today. It is very hard to tell you. It is about myself.

Yesterday I read an article by Sis Heyster. It might have been written for me personally. She writes that a girl my age becomes quiet inside because she is thinking about the wonders that are happening to her body.

I feel that, too. I think what is happening to me is wonderful. I don't mean only what can be seen on my body. I'm talking about all that is taking place inside. I never talk about these things with anyone. That is why I have to talk to myself about them. If only I had a girlfriend!

Thursday, 6 January, 1944

Dear Kitty,

My longing to talk to someone became so strong that somehow I chose Peter.

Peter's room has always seemed very comfortable to me. I never stayed long because I was afraid he might think me a bore. Peter is so shy and would never ask anyone to leave. I tried to think of an excuse to stay. I wanted to get him talking. He likes crossword puzzles, so I helped him with some. We sat on opposite sides of his little table.

It gave me a strange feeling to look into his deep blue eyes. He sat there with a laugh playing around his lips. I could see how nervous he was about how to act with me. I could see how shy he was. It made me feel very gentle. I kept meeting those dark eyes again and again. I wanted to ask him: Oh, tell me, tell me what is going on inside you. But the evening passed, and nothing happened.

Later I lay in bed and thought it over. I have made up my mind to spend more time with Peter. Somehow I will get him talking.

Don't think I'm in love with Peter—not a bit of it! If the Van Daans had a daughter instead of a son, I would want to be friends with her, too.

I woke up from a dream this morning. I dreamed that I was sitting with Peter. . . Wessel. Suddenly his eyes met mine. I looked into those fine, soft brown eyes for a long time. Then Peter said, "I wish I had known. I would have come to you before." And then I felt his cheek against mine. Oh, such a cool, kind cheek!

At this point, I woke up. I could still feel his cheek against mine and his brown eyes looking deep into my heart.

It is strange that I should see such vivid dreams here. I have seen both my grandmothers so clearly at night. Then there was Lies, who seemed to stand for the sufferings of all my friends and all Jews. And now Peter, my darling Peter.

Friday, 7 January, 1944

Dear Kitty,

The dream has really upset me. When Daddy kissed me good morning, I could have cried out, "Oh, if only you were Peter Wessel!" I had thought that I had forgotten him. I thought I didn't like him a bit any more. Now I think about him all the time. I keep saying to myself all day, "Oh, Peter, darling, darling Peter!"

Who can help me now? I must live on and pray that God will let Peter cross my path again when I get out of here. I love him with all my heart and soul.

Saturday, 22 January, 1944

Dear Kitty,

Why do people always try so hard to hide their true feelings? Why can't I be myself when I'm in other people's company? Why do we trust each other so little?

It seems as if I've grown up a lot since my dream the other night. Even my attitude toward the Van Daans is changing. I suddenly see the arguments in a different light.

How can I have changed so much? It's true that Mrs. Van Daan is by no means a nice person. She is selfish and sneaky, but you can reason with her if you don't irritate her. You have to be careful not to get on her bad side. Our problems with her could have worked out quite differently. We just needed to be open and friendly.

I want to start fresh. I don't want to always assume that the Van Daans are in the wrong. I want to discuss openly all the points on which we disagree. From today on, there will be no unkind gossip from me. I hope that I have found some insight and will use it well.

Monday, 24 January, 1944

Dear Kitty,

Whenever anyone at home or at school used to talk about sex, it was always something mysterious or disgusting. People whispered about it. If someone didn't understand, that person was laughed at. It struck me as very odd. I used to think, "Why are people so embarrassed by this subject?" But that was just the way it was. So I kept my mouth shut. Sometimes I talked with my girlfriends.

Once, after I had learned quite a lot, I spoke about it with my parents. Mother said, "Anne, let me give you some good advice. Never speak about this with boys. If they start talking about it, don't reply."

I remember well what my answer was. I said, "No, of course not! The very idea!" And there it stayed.

Peter Van Daan was never as weird about this subject as the boys at school. He never tried to get me talking. Mrs. Van Daan said that she never talked about these things with Peter. She guessed that her husband never did either. I guess she didn't know how much he knew. Because yesterday we talked. If it had been any other boy but Peter, I never would have looked at him again. But he talked about this subject quite normally. He didn't mean anything unpleasant. He put me at ease so that I could be normal too.

I knew I could not have discussed these things so openly with a girl. I'm wiser about one thing now. There really are people—boys, even!—who can discuss these things without making fun of them.

8 Peter

Saturday, 12 February, 1944

Dear Kitty,

The sun is shining, and the sky is a deep blue. There is a lovely breeze, and I'm longing—so longing—for everything. For freedom, for friends, to talk, to be alone. And I do long. . . to cry! I feel as if I'm going to burst.

I feel that it's spring within me. I feel it in my whole body and soul. I feel quite confused. I don't know what to read, what to write, what to do. I only know that I am longing. . . !

Sunday, 13 February, 1944

Dear Kitty,

A lot has changed for me since yesterday. I am still longing. But now something has happened that makes the longing a little easier to stand.

To my great joy—I will be honest about it—Peter keeps looking at me all the time. Not in the usual way. I don't know how, I just can't explain.

I used to think that Peter was in love with Margot. Yesterday I suddenly had the feeling that this was not so. I tried not to look at him too much, because when I did, he kept on looking too. It gave me a lovely feeling inside, but one which I must not feel too often.

Dear Kitty,

On Sunday evening, Peter had an argument with Dussel. The reason for it was not important, but Peter took it very much to heart. Today, when we were alone, he told me why. "You see," he said, "I don't talk easily. I get tongue-tied. I twist around what I'm going to say. Then I have to stop because I just can't find the words. That's what happened yesterday with Dussel. I used to have a bad habit. I wish I still had it. If I was angry with anyone, instead of arguing, I'd work it out with my fists. I realize that this way doesn't get me anywhere. That's why I admire you. You always know what to say to people. You are never shy."

I laughed to myself at this. "I can tell you, you're wrong," I said. "I usually say things very differently from how I mean to. Then I talk too much and too long, and that's just as bad."

I was very glad I was able to get Peter talking about himself. I felt very close to him, in a way I can remember only feeling with my girlfriends.

Friday, 18 February, 1944

Dear Kitty,

Whenever I go upstairs now, I hope that I will see "him." Because I now have something to look forward to, everything has become more pleasant.

Don't think I'm in love, because I'm not. But I do have the feeling that something fine can grow between us. I go up to see him all the time now. It's not like it used to be when he didn't know how to begin. It's just the opposite. He's still talking when I'm halfway out of the room.

Mother doesn't like it much. She always says I should not be a bother to him. Honestly, doesn't she think I have any sense? She always looks at me so strangely when I go into Peter's room. If she sees me coming downstairs, she asks me where I've been. I simply can't stand it.

Wednesday, 23 February, 1944

Dear Kitty,

It's lovely weather outside. In the morning I went to the attic with Peter. I lay on the floor and looked up at the blue sky and the bare chestnut tree. Raindrops were shining like silver on its branches. I breathed fresh air and watched birds glide on the wind.

We both felt that the spell should not be broken by words. We stayed there a long time.

Then Peter had to go up to the loft to chop wood. I watched him. I know he was showing off his strength. But I looked out the open window over the roofs of the city. The sky was a beautiful pale blue. "As long as this exists," I thought, "I cannot be unhappy."

As long as I can see this sky, this sunshine, I cannot be afraid or lonely. I feel connected with nature. As long as this exists, there will be comfort for every sorrow.

Sunday, 27 February, 1944

Dear Kitty,

From morning until night, I hardly do anything but think of Peter. I go to sleep with his face before my eyes. I dream about him, and he is still looking at me when I awake.

I feel that Peter and I are not as different as we may seem. For one thing, we both need a mother. His is too shallow and doesn't care what he thinks. Mine does care, but she is not a warm person.

Peter and I both wrestle with our feelings. When mine are hurt, I want to get away from it all. But, as that is impossible, I hide my feelings. I act noisy and throw my weight around. Peter, on the other hand, shuts himself off. He hardly talks at all. In this way, he hides his true self.

How and when will we reach each other? My common sense tells me to keep my feelings under control. I just don't know how long I can do it.

Peter Van Daan and Peter Wessel have grown into one Peter. He is beloved and good!

Kitty, I'm just like someone in love, who can only talk about her darling. And Peter really is a darling. When shall I be able to tell him so? Of course, I'll tell him only if he thinks I'm a darling too. I have no idea if or how much he likes me. In any case, we are getting to know each other a bit. I wish we dared to tell each other much more. Who knows, the time may come sooner than I think!

Wednesday, 1 March, 1944

Dear Kitty,

There has been another burglary. This one is more serious than the one last July. The thief used a key. We think he might be one of the men who works in our warehouse. Worse yet, he certainly heard Mr. Van Daan, and may even have seen him. Would he turn us in? It is all very scary.

Monday, 6 March, 1944

Dear Kitty,

I can tell by Peter's face that he thinks just as much as I do. Last night Mrs. Van Daan made a joke of it. "The thinker!" she said. Peter looked very embarrassed. I was about to explode with anger. Why can't these people keep their mouths shut?

It's horrible to see how lonely he is and not be able to do anything. It is so hard to get him to talk about himself. He has told me how his parents quarrel over everything. Poor Peter.

He says that he doesn't need friends. But it's just an act to hide his real feelings. Oh, Peter, if only I could help you! If only you would let me!

Tuesday, 7 March, 1944

Dear Kitty,

If I think now of my life in 1942, it seems so unreal. Peter remembers me from school. "Every time I saw you, you were surrounded by two or more boys and a bunch of girls. You were always laughing and always the center of everything," he said.

It was true. I had boyfriends at every turn. I had lots of friends. I was the pet of nearly all my teachers and spoiled by my parents. What more could one want?

Yet when I look back on that Anne, I see a fun person, but not a very deep person. She has nothing to do with the Anne of today. I'd like that sort of life again for a few days, maybe even a week. But at the end of that week, I would be bored silly. I don't want followers, but friends. I don't want to be liked for being cute and fun. I want to be admired for my deeds and my character.

I think of how much I have changed just since the New Year. Now, in the evening, I lie in bed and end my prayers with these words: "I thank you, God, for all that is good and dear and beautiful." I am filled with joy. Then I think about the good part of going into hiding. And, with my whole being, I think of Peter. I think of the feelings that are growing between us—which neither of us dares to name. I think of better times to come. I think of the beauty that is in the world.

This is one way in which Mother and I are so different. When I am feeling sad, she says,

"Think of the misery in the world. Be thankful that you are not sharing in it." I don't see how that can be right. Then how are you supposed to act when you are going through misery yourself? You are lost. There is always some beauty left— in nature, in freedom, in yourself. These can all help you. Look at these things and you find yourself again.

9 War Talk

Dear Kitty,

The people who have been giving us food coupons have been caught. We now just have our five ration cards. After tomorrow we will not have a scrap of fat left. To save bread, we have been eating fried potatoes for breakfast. Now those are gone, too. We shall have porridge instead. Tonight's supper is a hash made from cabbage preserved in a barrel. It's over a year old, and it stinks. Ugh! The thought of eating it makes me sick!

Everyone is complaining. Mrs. Van Daan thinks we're starving. She is afraid the Germans are winning the war. Mr. Van Daan is all right if he has something to smoke. If he doesn't, he complains about everything and quarrels with his wife. Even my mother talks of being hungry. But not Daddy. He says, "Everything's all right. I don't need anything. Give me my potatoes, and I will keep my mouth shut. Save some of my share for Elli. The war news is very promising."

Thursday, 16 March, 1944

Dear Kitty,

The weather is lovely. I'm going up to the attic in a minute.

I know why I am more restless than Peter. He has his own room where he can work, think, dream, and sleep. I am pushed around from one corner to another. That's why I spend so much time in the attic. There I can be by myself for a while. Still, I don't want to moan about it. I want to be brave. Thank goodness the others can't tell what I'm feeling. I'm growing cooler toward Mother every day. I'm not so close to Daddy, and I don't tell Margot anything. I'm all closed up. No one must know of the war going on inside me. War between longing and common sense. So far, sense has won; yet will longing prove stronger? Sometimes I fear that it will. Sometimes I hope that it will.

Oh, it is so hard not to say anything to Peter, but he must be the first to begin. There is so much I want to say. I've dreamed about it, but each day goes by and nothing has come true!

Sunday, 19 March, 1944

Dear Kitty,

Yesterday was a great day. I had decided to talk things out with Peter. We stood by the open window in his parents' room. It was evening, and

64

it was easier to talk in darkness than in bright light.

We told each other so much. I can't repeat it all, but it was so lovely. It was the most wonderful evening I have ever had in the "Secret Annex." We talked about our families. We talked about how we feel when we're alone with our thoughts. Oh, he was just as I thought! I said that there was not much difference between my noise and his silence. That I love peace and quiet, too, and have nothing for myself except my diary. We talked about how glad we are to have each other.

Wednesday, 22 March, 1944

Dear Kitty,

A shadow has fallen over my happiness. I've thought for a long time that Margot liked Peter a lot, too. I was afraid she might be very hurt.

"If I were in your place," I told her Monday, "I'd be jealous. I think it's rotten that you should be the odd one out."

"I'm used to that," she answered. She sounded bitter. But later that day, I got a letter from her. "I'm not jealous of you or Peter," she wrote. "I only feel a bit sorry that I haven't found anyone yet with whom to share my thoughts and feelings. Of course I'm not likely to for some time. But I am happy for you and Peter. Besides,

I am sure that he is not someone I would have chosen. I like Peter, but I think of him more as a younger brother. Please don't feel sorry for me or that you have done something wrong."

Her letter was very sweet. I still did not feel quite happy about it, and I don't think I will. We have exchanged more notes. It's much easier for me than talking. Meanwhile, it is getting more and more wonderful here. I believe, Kitty, that we may have a great love in the "Secret Annex." Don't worry, I'm not thinking of marrying him. I don't know what he will be like when he grows up. I don't know whether I attract him as a girl or whether he just wants a great friend. I'm just very glad that he's here. And I'm hoping for a kiss!

Monday, 27 March, 1944

Dear Kitty,

One very big chapter of our story in hiding should really be about the war. I haven't written much about it because it doesn't interest me very much. Everyone is always arguing about the news. It's simply stupid that there should be so many quarrels over it.

The people from outside bring us a lot of news that is not true. On the radio, the British talk constantly about their air attacks. And the Germans make a great business of lying. Still, we have the radio going all day. It gets boring. It's hard not to become a bore oneself.

Everyone is wondering about the Allied invasion. It has been a long time coming. Meanwhile, things outside are very bad. Bombs make the house shake. There is sickness in the city. Doctors dare not visit the sick. If they do, their cars are stolen. The Dutch have become a nation of thieves. If people leave their homes for five minutes, someone breaks in. Eight-year-old children break windows and steal what they can. There's one good thing in the middle of it all. As things get worse, the Dutch people are rising up against the Germans. Only a small number of them are on the wrong side.

Tuesday, 4 April, 1944

Dear Kitty,

For a long time I haven't had any idea of what I was studying for. The end of the war seems so far away. It's like a fairy tale. If it's not over by September, I won't go back to school. I'd be two years behind.

On Saturday, I felt miserable. I acted cheerful all day, but the moment I was alone I let myself go. I cried with my head on my arms. I sat on the bare floor with my knees drawn up. Then I came back to earth. I didn't want anyone to hear me crying. I began trying to talk some courage into myself. Just before 10:30, I fell into bed. It was over!

I must work. I want to become a journalist. I know I can write. A couple of my stories are good, and there's a lot in my diary that speaks. But do I have real talent? I suppose we shall see. If I can't write books and magazine articles, I can always write for myself.

I don't want to live the same sort of life as Mother and Mrs. Van Daan. So many women do their work and then are forgotten. I must have something besides a husband and children.

I want to go on living even after my death!

10 The Biggest Scare!

Tuesday, 11 April, 1944

Dear Kitty,

My head aches. I hardly know where to start. On Sunday evening Peter and I went to the attic together. So that we could sit comfortably, we took a few cushions. We sat on a narrow box, leaning against other boxes. Mouschi was our chaperone.

Around a quarter to nine, Mr. Van Daan whistled. He asked if we had one of Dussel's cushions. We both jumped up and went back downstairs with the cushion and the cat.

Then there was trouble. Dussel made a big fuss about his cushion. He was afraid there might be fleas in it. Peter and I put two hard brushes in his bed to get even. We had a good laugh over it.

Our fun didn't last long. At 9:30, Peter knocked softly on the door. He asked Daddy if he would come upstairs and help him with a hard English sentence. "Anyone can see through that one," I said to Margot. "Something is up."

I was right. Someone was breaking into the warehouse. The men were all downstairs in a flash. The women stayed upstairs and waited.

A few minutes later, we heard a loud bang. Then silence. We sat quietly, afraid. Were the men fighting the burglars? Ten o'clock: footsteps on the stairs. Daddy, white and nervous, came in, followed by Van Daan. "Lights out. Get upstairs quietly. The police will be coming!"

There was no time to be scared. The lights went out; we went upstairs. "What happened? Tell us!" There was no one to tell us. The men had gone back down. When they returned, two of them kept watch at Peter's open window. The door and the cupboard were shut. Only then did we hear the story:

Peter had heard two loud bangs on the landing. He ran downstairs and saw that a hole had been knocked in the door. That was when he came up to warn Daddy. When the men entered the warehouse, they saw the burglars. They were making the hole wider. Van Daan shouted, "Police!"

The burglars ran. The men tried to put a board over the hole so that the police would not notice it. But just then, a man and a woman walked by. They shined a flashlight into the hole. It lit up the whole warehouse. So now the four men had to switch from police to burglars. Peter opened doors and windows in the offices. Daddy threw things on the floor. Finally, the four of them came back upstairs.

We sat there in the dark, waiting. At 11:15 there was noise downstairs. I could hear everyone's breath, but no one moved. Footsteps in the house, in the private office, in the kitchen. Then. . . on the stairs. Now I couldn't even hear breathing. Someone rattled the cupboard door. "Now we are lost," I thought. I could see us all being taken away by the Gestapo that very night. The cupboard rattled again. The footsteps withdrew. Then nothing. We were safe—so far.

We passed the night in terror. It was all but impossible to sleep. If the police came back, they would find us. If they were good Dutch people, they would help us. If they were for Hitler. . .

"Destroy the radio," Mrs. Van Daan said.

"They will find Anne's diary," Daddy said.

"Burn it then," Mrs. Van Daan said.

Except for when the police rattled the cupboard, this was my worst moment. "Not my diary!" I said. "If my diary goes, then I go with it!" But Daddy didn't answer.

In the morning, Daddy phoned Koophuis. By 11 o'clock, everything was explained. The couple with the flashlight turned out to be our vegetable man and his wife. "I did not tell the police," the vegetable man told Henk. "I didn't think it was the thing to do. I don't know anything, but I guess a lot." Clearly he guessed that we're here. He always brings the potatoes during the lunch hour. Such a nice man!

The night watchman, Mr. Slagter, had also seen the hole. It was he who called the police. Miep found a note he left under the door.

None of us has ever been in such danger as that night. God truly protected us. Kraler was angry. He said we had been careless. No one ought to go downstairs in a case like that. Henk reminded us that we are Jews in hiding. We are chained to one spot, without any rights.

Who has made us different from other people? We can never become just Dutch, or just English. We are Jews. We want to remain Jews. But we are people, too.

Be brave! God has never deserted our people. All through the ages there have been Jews. They have suffered, but it has made them strong.

That night, I felt that I was going to die. I was as ready as a soldier in battle. I would have died for my country. Now that I have been saved, my first wish after the war is that I may become Dutch. I love this country, I love the people. I want to work here. I will reach this goal even if I have to write to the Queen herself.

I am becoming free of my parents, young as I am. I face life with more courage than Mother. I have a truer feeling for what is right. I know what I want. I have a religion, and I have love. Let me be myself, that is enough. I know that I'm a woman, a woman with inner strength and plenty of courage.

If God lets me live, I will do more than Mother ever has done. I will be somebody. I will work in the world and for humankind!

Sunday morning, just before eleven o'clock,
16 April, 1944

Darlingest Kitty,

Remember yesterday's date. It is a very special day for me. Surely it is a great day for every girl when she has her first kiss.

Yesterday evening at eight o'clock, I was sitting with Peter on his couch. His arm went up around my shoulder. Now, this has happened before, but we have never been so close as yesterday. He held me firmly against him. Already my heart was beating faster. My head was on his shoulder, and his against it. Oh, it was so lovely! He stroked my cheek and my arm and played with my curls. I can't tell you, Kitty, the feeling that ran through me!

We got up. I stood beside him. How it came about so suddenly, I don't know. But before we went downstairs, he kissed my cheek. I ran downstairs without looking around. I longed for today, when I could write it all down!

11 D-Day

Dear Kitty,

I've never forgotten my dream of Peter Wessel last January. I can still feel his cheek against mine and remember that beautiful feeling.

Sometimes I have had that same feeling here with Peter. Yesterday we were sitting on the couch with our arms around each other. Suddenly, the ordinary Anne slipped away. In her place was a second Anne. This is not the Anne who is always talking and joking. This Anne just wants to be gentle.

I pressed closely against him. A wave of feeling came over me. Tears came to my eyes. Did he notice? Did he feel the same way I did? Does he know that there are two Annes before him? I do not know.

At 8:30, I stood up and went to the window, where we always say good-bye. I was still trembling. I was still Anne number two. He came towards me. I flung my arms around his neck. My lips met his, and we pressed them together. In a whirl we were locked in each other's arms.

Peter has touched my feelings more deeply than anyone before—except in my dreams. He has turned me inside out.

Oh, Peter, what have you done to me? I am only 14. I am afraid of myself. I am afraid that in my longing I am giving myself too quickly. Oh, it is hard, always battling with one's heart and one's good sense!

Tuesday, 2 May, 1944

Dear Kitty,

I have spoken to Daddy about Peter.

"I thought you were just pals," he said. He doesn't think that what we are doing is wrong, but that we must be careful. "It's different from normal times, when you are free to see other boys and girls. Here, if you want to get away, you can't. You see each other all the time. Be careful, Anne, and don't take it too seriously. I don't want you to go upstairs so much in the evenings any more."

I don't want that. It's not only because I like being with Peter. I want to show Daddy that I trust Peter. I can't do that if I stay downstairs. No, I'm going!

Wednesday, 3 May, 1944

Dear Kitty,

No war news this week. I am beginning to believe that there will be an invasion after all.

England and the United States can't let the Russians do all the fighting. For that matter, the Russians aren't even doing anything right now.

As you can guess, we often ask ourselves, "What is the use of this war? Why can't people live peacefully together?"

Yes, why do they spend millions on the war, and yet there's not a penny available for health care, art, or poor people? No one has come up with a good answer yet.

I don't believe that the big men, the leaders alone, caused the war. I think the little men are just as guilty. Otherwise the peoples of the world would have stopped war long ago. People have an urge to destroy, to kill. Until there is a great change in all humankind, wars will be fought. Everything people have built will be destroyed, and they will have to begin all over again.

Even so, I have never given up. I think of our hiding as a dangerous but interesting adventure. I am young and strong and cheerful. Every day I am growing inside. Nature is beautiful, the people around me are interesting, and the end of the war will come. Why then, should I give up?

Friday, 5 May, 1944

Dear Kitty,

Daddy is not happy with me. He thought that after our talk on Sunday I wouldn't go upstairs every evening. He is making it very hard for me. I will talk to him today. This is roughly what I want to say:

"I believe, Daddy, that you are not happy with me. I suppose you want me to be just as a 14-year-old should be. But that's where you're wrong.

"Since we came here, I have not had an easy time. If you knew how unhappy I felt, how lonely, you would understand that I want to be with Peter!

"I am now able to live on my own, without Mother's help or yours. You can laugh at me and not believe me, but that can't hurt me. I am only telling you this because I thought that otherwise you might think I was being sneaky. I don't have to explain what I do to anyone but myself.

"When I had problems, none of you helped me. You only scolded me about being so loud and foolish. I acted that way only so that I wouldn't be hurting all the time. Now the battle is over. I have won! I am free. I don't need a mother any more. This battle has made me strong.

"And now I will go my own way. You must not see me as 14, for all these troubles have made me older. I will not be sorry for what I do. I will act as I think I must. Either forbid me to go upstairs, or trust me. Then leave me in peace!"

Sunday, 7 May, 1944

Dear Kitty,

Daddy and I had a long talk yesterday. I cried a lot, and he joined in. On Friday I wrote what I explained to you in a letter. I put it in his pocket before supper. Margot told me that he was very upset for the rest of the evening. (I was upstairs doing the dishes.)

Yesterday he told me that I had done him a great wrong. "You, Anne, who have received such love from your parents, can say we have not helped you? We have always been ready to help you. We have always defended you. How can you talk of feeling no responsibility to us? Maybe you didn't mean it that way, but that is what you wrote."

Oh, this is the worst thing I have ever done! I was only showing off. I was just trying to appear big, so that he would respect me. Certainly I have had problems. But to accuse Daddy, who has done so much for me—no, that was too low for words.

It's right that my pride has been shaken. I was becoming much too taken up with myself again. The way Daddy has forgiven me makes me feel ashamed of myself. No, Anne, you still have much to learn.

I want to start over with him. That can't be hard, now that I have Peter. With him to help me, I can and will!

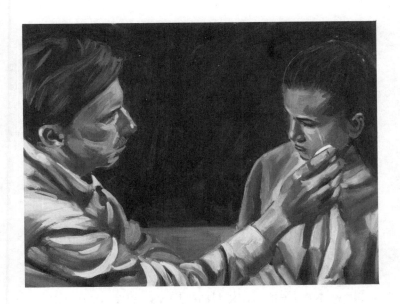

I'm not alone any more. I have love. I have my
books, my stories, and my diary. I'm not ugly or
stupid. But I want to have good character.

Yes, Anne, that letter was too hard, and it was
untrue. To think that you were even proud of it! I
will take Daddy as my example, and I will
improve.

Monday, 22 May, 1944

Dear Kitty,

On Saturday Daddy lost a bet with Mr. Van
Daan. The invasion still has not come. All of
Amsterdam, all of western Europe, talks about
the invasion day and night. We talk, we make
bets. . . we hope.

Many good Dutch people are angry at England for waiting so long. The English are not cowards. They are fighting for their own country. Why should they be blamed for not helping us? The invasion will come, but England and the United States will decide when.

To our great horror and sadness, we hear that many Dutch people have now turned against the Jews. They blame us for giving secrets to the Germans. They say it's our fault that they are punished. But the Germans have ways of making people talk. Can a person who is being tortured always remain silent?

Now we hear talk that Jews who came here from Germany will not be allowed to stay here after the war. The Dutch welcomed them, but when Hitler is gone they will be sent back to Germany.

Is this right? Why, then, are we fighting this war? We always hear that we're fighting together for freedom, for truth. Are Jews worth less than others?

I can't understand why the Dutch should judge us like this. They are a good, honest people. They gave us such a warm welcome, and now they turn their backs on us. I only hope that this hatred of the Jews will pass. I hope that the Dutch will not lose their sense of right. Otherwise, we will have to leave Holland. We will have to move on again with our little bundles. We will have to leave this beautiful country.

I love Holland. I hoped that it might become my home. I still hope it will.

Friday, 26 May, 1944

Dear Kitty,

I have not been so low in months. Not even the burglary made me feel so broken. On Thursday, our vegetable man was taken away by the Germans. He was caught hiding two Jews in his house. Every day good people are dragged off to prison. Anyone who betrays the Germans does not know what may happen from one day to the next.

This man is a great loss to us, too. Elli and Miep cannot bring us our share of potatoes. The only thing to do is to eat less. We shall have no breakfast at all. We're going to be hungry, but anything is better than being discovered.

Tuesday, 6 June, 1944

Dear Kitty,

"This is D-day," said the announcement on the English radio. "This is the day." The invasion has begun! English and U.S. troops have landed in France. There is hard fighting. Planes are flying back and forth, carrying troops and supplies.

Oh, Kitty, the best part of the invasion is that I feel that friends are coming! The Germans have oppressed us for so long! U.S. General Eisenhower said today, "The year 1944 is the year of victory." Perhaps, Margot says, I may be able to go back to school this fall after all.

12 Hope for Freedom

Dear Kitty,

Another birthday has gone by. Now I'm 15. I received quite a lot of presents, mostly food and books.

There is still excellent news of the invasion. The Allies are dug in on the French coast. Any Dutch people who call the English cowards deserve a good shaking.

Wednesday, 14 June, 1944

Dear Kitty,

My head is full of so many things today. I'm not as conceited as so many people seem to think. I know my faults better than anyone. The difference is that I also know that I want to improve.

Why, then, do people say that I'm a know-it-all? Is it so, or is it maybe that the others don't know very much? I know that sounds odd, but it really isn't. Take Mrs. Van Daan, one of my accusers. To put it plainly, she's stupid. Stupid people usually can't take it if others know more than they do.

The worst part is that I am harder on myself than anyone. Then Mother adds her bit of advice. The pile of sermons becomes so big that I become rude. I start arguing with people. I know it sounds silly, but it's true. I'm often so hard on myself that I long for a word of comfort. I need someone who can give me sound advice and also draw out some of my real self. I keep looking, but I haven't found anyone yet.

I know you'll think, "What about Peter?" It's like this, Kitty: Peter loves me only as a friend. He grows more loving each day, but something seems to hold us back. Sometimes I wonder if I really ever longed for him so terribly. Yet when I don't go up to see him for two days, I need him more than ever. Peter is good and sweet, but there's a lot about him that's not right for me. He does not care for religion. He talks too much about things that don't interest me. And why does he still keep his inner self hidden? Why am I never allowed there?

Tuesday, 27 June, 1944

Dear Kitty,

The mood has changed. The news is wonderful. The English and U.S. troops are advancing in the west, the Russians in the east. They are taking lots of German prisoners. Daddy and Van Daan think we should be free by October.

Mrs. Van Daan has even stopped talking about suicide. No one takes her seriously anyway. She has no character. The worst thing about her is that she makes Peter rude and everyone else grumpy.

Dear Kitty,

We have a book from the library called *What Do You Think of the Modern Young Girl?* The author does not have much good to say about "the youth of today." She thinks that young people could make a better world. Instead they keep themselves busy with things that aren't important.

There were places where I felt this writer was talking to me personally. I don't think she was fair. Anyone who knows me can see that I know myself very well. I can see what's good and bad about myself without making excuses. I understand what Daddy means when he says, "All children must look after their own upbringing." Parents can put them on the right paths, but a person's character lies in his or her own hands.

Daddy did all he could to make me a "good girl." He never realized that my fight to be myself was more important than anything else. I wanted him to see me not as "a girl," but as Anne. He

never understood that. This is why I could never really share my thoughts with him.

I knew that I was pushing him away. I couldn't have done anything else. Because if I had let him criticize me for trying to be myself, I would have lost my confidence. Yet I still feel badly about that letter I wrote him. Oh, how hard it is to be really strong and brave in every way!

Yet I think far more about Peter than about Daddy. I know that I won him instead of him winning me. I painted a picture of him in my mind. I saw him as a quiet, sensitive boy who needed my love and friendship. We have talked about the most private things. Yet we still have not touched on those thoughts that fill my heart and soul. I still don't know what to make of Peter. Is he shallow, or does he still feel shy, even around me? I can see him growing more and more in love with me. I have let him get close to me. Now he clings to me. For now, I don't see any way of shaking him off and putting him on his own feet.

"Youth is more lonely than old age." I read this saying somewhere, and I have found it to be true. Do grown-ups have a harder time here than we do? No. Older people have formed their ideas about everything. They act on these ideas without thinking. It's twice as hard for us young ones to hold our ground. It's even more so in times like these. Ideals are being broken, people are showing their worst side. It's hard to know whether to believe in truth and justice and God.

We are much too young for such problems, but we have to face them all the time. After a while we think we've found an answer, but then the facts bring our answer to nothing. That's the hard thing about these times. Ideals, dreams, and hopes rise within us, only to meet the truth and be broken.

It's really a wonder that I haven't dropped all my ideals. In spite of everything, I still believe that people are really good at heart. I see the world being turned into a desert. I can feel the world's sufferings. Yet if I look up into the heavens, I think that it will all come right. This cruelty will end, and peace will return.

Tuesday, 1 August, 1944

Dear Kitty,

I'm a little bundle of contradictions. I am like two people: the one I show others and the one I keep to myself. The first is all the bad things for which I'm well known—"never giving in, always knowing best, getting in the last word." The second no one knows about. That's my own secret.

I've talked before of being two people. One half is always cheerful, in high spirits. I make fun of everything; I take everything lightly. This side usually pushes away the other, deeper, purer side. No one knows this side of Anne. That's why most people find me hard to take.

I hate having to tell you this, but why not, if it's true? My lighter side will always be too quick for my deeper side. That's why it will always win. You can't know how often I've tried to push this Anne away. After all, she's only half of me. But it doesn't work, and I know why.

I'm scared that everyone who knows me will discover this deeper side. I'm afraid they'll laugh at me. The "lighter" Anne is used to being laughed at. The "deeper" Anne is too weak to stand it.

This is why the nice Anne is never present in company but is almost always around when I'm alone. I know just how I'd like to be, but I'm only like that for myself. I must admit that it hurts me. I try so hard to change, but I'm always fighting against a stronger enemy.

I keep on trying to find a way of becoming what I would so like to be. I could be that way if. . . there weren't any other people living in the world.

Epilogue

Here Anne Frank's diary ends. On August 4, 1944, the Germans broke into the Secret Annex. Someone—probably one of the warehouse workers—had told them of the hiding place. Anne and the others were taken away and separated from one another. What happened to Anne afterward has been pieced together from the stories of people who knew her. She died in a concentration camp early in March, 1945.

Two months later, the war in Europe ended. Of the people who had lived in the Secret Annex, the only survivor was Anne's father, Otto Frank. He made his way back to Amsterdam. He found that Miep Van Santen and Elli Vossen had saved some notebooks and papers. Among them was Anne's diary.